Elegy for My Tongue

Elegy for My Tongue

Saba Husain

Terrapin Books

© 2023 by Saba Husain
Printed in the United States of America.
All rights reserved.
No part of this book may be reproduced in any manner, except for brief quotations embodied in critical articles or reviews.

Terrapin Books
4 Midvale Avenue
West Caldwell, NJ 07006

www.terrapinbooks.com

ISBN: 978-1-947896-68-0
Library of Congress Control Number: 2023941403

First Edition

Cover art: Sydney Kornegay
photograph

Cover design: Diane Lockward

for Ammi and Aboo
and those before
and after

Contents

The Resettlement	3

۱

An Anthology of Urdu Verse	7
Night Ghazal	8
Ya Allah Ya Rabb	10
Here I Come, Lord	11
My Karachi and the Sea	12
A Nearly Dried-Up Woman	14
The Tomb of the Saint Lal Shahbaz Qalandar at Sehwan Sharif	15
Silence Is a Two-Syllable Word	16
Thank You, Big Sister, for Buying a Rose	18
The Geometry of an Ellipse	19
To My Mother for Bearing	20

۲

The Golden Racemes	25
The Remuneration	26
At the Shrine of Favors Ask for Humility	28
The Missing Planet	29
Texas Tag	30
The Fertilized Garden	31
The Kite	32
With Gratitude to My Great Grandfather, Mianbhai Abdul 1859-1922	33
The Bid	35
A Healing Tree	37

۳

The Prayer	41
The Last Qawwali	42
Elegy for My Tongue	43
The Clothesline	44
On Dry Ground	46

After Inhabiting Spaces Where Nothing That Mattered Could Grow	48
The Reluctant Mourner for the Refugee Mother	49
Consider the Day	50
Urdu as Motif: An Elegy in Three Voices	51
The Immeasurable Weight of Light	53
On Being Asked What Language I Write In	54
The Reunion at Khayaban-e-Khushi, Karachi	56

ر

The Artificial Lake	61
When December Runs into a Tree of Gold	62
Like Homemade	63
Back then Houston was like any other city,	64
By the Broken Obelisk for Dr. King Outside Rothko Chapel in Houston	65
Found on the Richter Scale	66
Truth Be Told I Did Not Care to Be Taken Aside	68
Texas Toll	69
Thresholds	70
Shehr Ashob or Misfortunes of a City	72
The *Soandhaapun* of Rain on Dry Earth	74

ھ

The Tree by the Garden Gate	77
Found Anthem	78
Related to the Viscera	80
Thirty Minute Oil Change in a Free Country	81
Parable	82
The Unlikeliness of Empty Spaces	83
Let's Talk About the Leaves	84
Texas Blooms	86
The Donning	87
I Close my Eyes and Stand Under the Tallow	89
Acknowledgments	91
About the Author	95

تو مجھے بھول بھی جائے تو کوئی بات نہیں
میں تری یاد کو جینے کا سہارا کر لوں

ہارون شاہد

That you should forget me is of no consequence
I will turn your memory into a reason for my existence
—Haroon Shahid

The Resettlement

We picked zinnias the day before leaving,
and armfuls of marigolds
from a farm refugees had sown.

Late September warmed
the beans on the poles, and somewhere
between the kale's neat rows
and tomorrow, childhood
homes were left behind.

We worked fast under the sun,
learned where to nip the blooms,
arranged petals in blue glass jars,
threaded needles through fleshy stems
for garlands.

We clung to a music of our own,
traced henna on our palms,
basked in bouquets.
No one said goodbye.

1

An Anthology of Urdu Verse

The last time someone spoke *Middle Eastern*
on a domestic flight,
an arrest was made mid-air.
                                       I placed
            my copy
of Urdu poems
with translation
on my lap,
so only the English was visible to the woman
seated next to me,
and I veiled the title with my hands,
and was ashamed of my fear
                                until the world
of this other

language took over
and I understood what hunger
has to do with sour teeth and bitter tongues.

I almost forgot where I sat
and raised the book
                            to the level
of the folding tray,
glanced out the window
to where a deep rose seeped into the seamless horizon,
                and when my neighbor turned
her face towards me—
                        she was ordinary.

Night Ghazal

Those last nights of Ramzaan: one night like a thousand.
Clot to man, pen to read. Read, read the night.

In the window, the moon raises its guilty face.
My face in the mirror, a facet of the night.

Fleeting wings, sweating skin, and nothing else
except hell's want—a chasm that blindsides night.

Of angels, of sinners, of doors opened wide,
a prayer for refuge unrolling on my lips.

A bed of marigolds for a saint's shrine,
regretting all the nights I missed on other nights.

Call me to you, I said, my forehead to the mat,
but my heart had drifted continents, seized the night.

Stringed sandalwood, beads smoothed to a shine,
in the recesses of a drawer, left for lost that night.

The calls from minarets, like plaintiffs they arrive
and draw crimson silk immersed in night.

Tired shoulders holding sky on upright palms,
a beggar spreads her cloth for mercy tonight.

Kohl is easily smudged, Saba, can you not see
what's left in your cup—the dregs of the night.

Ya Allah Ya Rabb

June bugs are performing rituals of birth
and death; it is not June, nor has the clock
sprung the hour, but counts each long
drawn breath of a mother battling a cancer
that marinated in her breasts, then skewered
her lungs before staking out her head.
She utters what fragments of prayer she can,
and she'd curse if she had the strength—
for the lost cause of a homeland razed by war,
a worthless spouse who died on her,
her children at the mercy of foster care,
and this new country whose earth she will become
yet fails to grasp its cold, cold tongue.
June bugs scratch at the kitchen door,
spin on their backs like crazies gone too long
under the heat of a light bulb.

Here I Come, Lord

We drove an hour from Jeddah to Mecca,
and there was nothing modest
about blank skies and shifting sands,
a highway blasted through rock
and black hill, an animal carcass—
white-gold under an obsequious sun,
and not much else, except,

here I come, Lord, here I come.

At one point the ascent curved, giving
a brief glimpse of the city, glittering
like Youssef to Zuleika in the desert,
then cloaked once again in the immense
darkness that fell, Ammi and I
unaccustomed to covering our heads,
and Aboo's old Cressida
cameling through impossible passes.

The descent into the valley, invariably
after dusk, floodlights replacing the sun,
fossil fuels comingling with attar-water
of rose, silver-speckled sandalwood
rosary between finger and thumb,
and bare-soled pilgrims converging
in concentric circles around the black
Kaaba embroidered in gold,
here I am, Lord.

My Karachi and the Sea

The wind from the sea, stench of fish on the beach,
glides through the chinks in the torn screen,
morning gropes for rooms and stairs,
hair on forehead like drowned petals,
skin tantalized by sweat
sends prayers,

and not far from the gated homes,
bus smog lingers.
The homeless sleep on footpaths
like bluebottles littering sand.
The green shrine's steps lose water's edge.

Here is exhaustion on graveled night,
dreams of sweetened saffron.
Under the Tamarind tree
the old bazaar reels
from vendors' drawn out calls,
crackling snacks, cars circling
like starving dogs,
fuming generators, light bulbs
singeing decades of grime, limbs
groveling on asphalt.

And on the street that climbs back up,
bougainvillea clings to walls.
A water truck stops to take its fill.
Morning staggers

onto side streets and lawns,
onto driveways, through windows and doors,
into rooms lulled by the sea,

while fish die on the beach.

A Nearly Dried-Up Woman

after Alice Oswald

It's a likeness of gray rain,
distant sounds of singing,
a clicking of dry grass,
of chaffed grain, scattered
fields, children running.

A speechless, broken old woman
shows her hazel-eyed girl the okra that grows
on the stalk. An unintelligible monotone,
a throat clearing rustle, distant, dry grass.

Little shufflings of night slippers tripping
approaching a low burning glint of stones:
a man in full night gear slithering
over a river of limestone and bones.

Her sun-wrinkled arm missing,
and both legs from the knee down,
eyes closing on the blue of a drone.

The Tomb of the Saint Lal Shahbaz Qalandar at Sehwan Sharif

Let's not lament the blue and gold tessellations on white
tiles, or shining marble stained with the blood bath
of penitent pilgrims. Let's not lament. A dome
stands testament to a mother's gaze as she
scours the last outposts of the city.
There will be other days after
the floors are swept and the
children are laid down in
the landscape, and the
white-haired woman
dances to her pain,
hems of her red
robe swirling to
the chorus of
wooden reeds.

Silence Is a Two-Syllable Word

God taught Adam: tree, fruit, leaf, snake.
A woman learns early on, the weight of things to come.

She lets it lay heavy against her skin,
reside inside her body.

Patience is a two-syllable word.

In dusty orchards
across the border
where unexploded ordnance
is mistaken for dried pomegranates,

women deliver loaded
poems from behind the screens
of shuttlecock burkas.

Take that—

How easy or hard is it to lay
a finger on
the precise moment when
sweet syrup turns acrid.

A song can be sung
with a stone-dead face.

The tongue, irreverent as it is,
plays the game.

Thank You, Big Sister, for Buying a Rose

Little boy, I could not find you
amidst the throngs.

I did not look you in the eye
when I rolled
my window down
to drop a few rupees
for the single stem
you offered me
at a traffic signal.

The flower you slid
from your hand
to mine—

white gardenia
sweating inside dismembered
red petals, barely held
the semblance of a rose.

On Karachi's polluted streets,
a cluster fell apart
in my palms.

The Geometry of an Ellipse

As if the light from the zodiac   spilling
onto rose floors   and a clock chiming
on a waltzing concourse
were not enough   how many

have stood   in the whispering gallery
and stuttered   into silence
when they heard the words   *you belong*
from the corners   of its walls

and were transported   to childhood
counting to ten   playing under lemon trees
anticipating   more afternoons

roamed the red brick streets   Mughal forts
   lush gardens   Lahore
and held on   to its ditches and lanes

till they found themselves   standing
under   a domed ceiling
in Grand Central

To My Mother for Bearing

And the pains of childbirth drove her to the trunk of a palm tree. She said, "Oh, I wish I had died before this, and was in oblivion, forgotten."
—Surah Maryam 19:23 The Qur'an

    I

1947: On the deck of a ship that sails
from India to Pakistan,
my mother is in her mother's arms.

The surge of an ocean carries them.

Six years old, on a dirt road.
Snakes cross her path.

On the bus ride to school,
children from a colonial order
push her aside.

    II

I scream for my mother from a birthing bed.
The world is crimson, raw, and glistening.

My bones bloom
like a desiccated lotus
left overnight
in an earthen vessel
filled to the brim
with water.

III

To face an uncertain passage,
to trust
the light
for forcing sight
into eyes
and air for pushing breath
into lungs,

knowing this was but the beginning
of a great descent.

۲

The Golden Racemes

O you, humming a forgotten melody before your long flight home,
don't forget—when desires become obsolete, return in a dream.

Confide in me, Dad, under the laburnum tree,
the sun is mild and warms the oranges
sunning on the old bench. Tell me
before the afternoon's gone how you were
your grandmother's cherished grandson.

I've seen my granddaughter's head
protrude into the world.
I've known the instance
when my grandson's radiance
seeped into the marrow of my bones.

The laburnum forgets to bloom some years,
but its trunk has taken on the likeness of a bard.
The oranges will always be plenty in winter
and the garden will be petaled
with orange rind flowers.

Sing to me in your graveled voice,
lilting like her last request: the song
you sang in your fourteen-year-old voice
when you stood by your grandmother's bed.

The Remuneration

1928: Grandfather, a civil servant
in British India, surveyed Sirsa District on camel back.

Irrigated fields reaped oats and barley in autumn,
mustard and grams in spring.

With the drought, locust burrowed their eggs,
pushing them six to nine inches in the sand.

With no crops, nor planes to dust the fields, villagers were told
they'd be paid the weight of locust eggs.

Grandfather's photographic memory yielded an abundance
of detail in the memoir he left

but nowhere near the count of locust eggs
peasants collected and turned in.

Tilyar birds fed on the pests,
gained protection on the hunting trail.

Now: I search for the bird
    all over the web,
but only the namesake
lake comes back,
and a video set to Euro-techno.

Tilyar group
           and break above the lake.
Black specks
      in unpredictable formations
aim as one
for some unreachable place,
then pulse to life in assigned spaces—
typed characters on a page.

At the Shrine of Favors Ask for Humility

Great grandfather was paralyzed
on the left side of his body
by a stroke of ill luck.

He lost the use of an arm and leg
at a time when a long-awaited
government post opened up
for the first time to the colonized
citizens of India.

On an oxcart lined with a mattress,
he made weekly trips to a tomb
where a saint lay interred.

Often, he was accompanied
by his adolescent son
who recalled the shrine at Burhanpur:
how pilgrims left their shoes at the door,
entered barefoot out of respect.

How, before entering the shrine,
he would go down on his knees
to remove his father's shoes.

The Missing Planet

Oblivious to the red blood moon,
we strung the universe on a wire hanger
in order of distance from the sun:

Neptune's swing entangled
Saturn's rings, and sent Jupiter
spinning towards Mars.

While the lunar jaw dropper was witnessed
from Sri Lanka to California,
I counted generations on my fingertips,
and imagined faces I'd never met
turned towards the sky.

In another time and age I'd be
on my knees at the spectacle,
having dallied enough nights on my driveway
to know a Texas sky.

Grandson, hold on to the blue green
sphere you plucked from your mobile,
tuck the Earth under your pillow,
let the moon orbit your eyes.

Texas Tag

On the road to Katy, on a highway stretched
like a Cajun song, the generosity of the sun
amplifies virgin fields where grazing cows
set idyllic tones for suburban outposts of stone
columned entrances and waterfront dreams.

The light, always the light, shifting over a green
layout of an American cosmos; trace and repeat
master plan coveted cul-de-sac Fourth-of-July
streets, mother, father, high school team,
mailbox, bus stop, crispy treats, a dinner
of desiccated mash and meat,

a nest unraveling in an old oak tree,
accordion unfolding,
one hand on wheel, flicker of speed,
halcyon cloud-shadows
on an open field—and the toll.

The Fertilized Garden

Under tallow trees
we push swings
for grandbabies
born here,
but always close:
Karachi.

In the garden where Grandfather planted snapdragons
and phlox bloomed in winter,
                      a gulmohar tree flamed,
we trod on bougainvillea
                      petals amidst remains,
fractured brick
                      where wall met sunset,
a fallen guava's
                smashed pink flesh,
and slumber breaking koel birds
                      silent on barbed wire
like jasmine
garlands threaded for tombs.

The Kite

My grandson found a kite in the back of a closet.

On the first day of spring,
                        a cold front
whipped the wind through boughs
            and scattered the contents
of overflowing recycling bins.

This is what it means to be in the now;
                    release a kite to the wind,
feel the tug of a string,
his small face turns up,
                all fascination to the sky.

What is happiness, what is the now?
                        Two spaces
later, we're already (the) past.
            We are, and we are, and then we are
a murky were. We were
unable to resurrect
                bits caught in the tree line.

With Gratitude to My Great Grandfather, Mianbhai Abdul 1859-1922

whose purpose in compiling a book
in English was to dispel any
unfortunate misunderstandings
against a Muslim minority sect
into which he was born in British India.

My father gave me the one copy that survived:
a faded xerox, hard bound.

When there is nothing, there will be words.
First edition: 500 print.

Bio: *the compiler is a distinguished scholar
who commenced his career as the headmaster of a high school
and retired as a government servant.
He received Honorarium for writing
Ethnographical Survey notes in 1906 A.D.*

Great grandfather,
I hold your words in my hands.

21 sources listed in Appendix G, but I
cling to your remarks based on personal observation.

*And to those who say that the study of English
conduces to a loss of faith—I refer them to the speaker
at the Educational Conference of Surat, 1918…*

Great grandfather, the year is 2020
and there's explaining to be done:

*the fear's baseless, besides, it is doubtful
whether in these days of freedom and advancement,
the suppression of journalism and education will be effective.*

Errata: *Due to my ill health and inability
to supervise the correction of proofs personally,
it is hoped the reader will excuse any mistakes.*

Appendix L:
*I leave this [appendix] incomplete
for future writers.*

The Bid

A buyer upped the offer
for the broken brick driveway,
the termite gnawed doors.

In summer, latched windows in high ceilinged rooms
were lifted. Cool breezes
floated across the house.
In winter, our teeth chattered
on the icy floors of those same rooms.

Mice used to play in the halls;
Aunt J secretly fed them crumbs.

She lived there most of her life.

The lemon tree planted long ago,
the verandah with the bamboo shades where the black dog
slept out his days, the fruit vendor with his cart,
remained the same. We grew.

As children we knew of a room in the back of the house
where the doorway opened onto a field.
Here, water buffalo were tethered,
and we saw the birth of a calf.

On some days we carried the milk to the churn
and watched it turn into white butter.
We spread it on bread, ate, and ran back out.

Aunt sits on a terrace in my cousin's house.
A man sells candy floss to children in the street below.

It's a mild winter in Lahore.
The sun is out but she tires
from the hum of traffic, wants to return inside.

A Healing Tree

There's the cold damp earth,
the underbrush of grass and leaves.
Aunt returns to the hospital bed.
She's a willow tree. Last I sat down with her,
she was eyeing the chocolate éclair
over the lemon tart on her plate.
She sways.
We sop tendrils in tears.

٣

The Prayer

Before dawn, before dawn, the minarets,
footsteps crossing the blue-tiled floor,
vortex of stars spilling from a circle,
waves lapping at my bedroom door.

One crow, then more, in the pebbled courtyard.
New voices join in: here's to dawn, to dawn;
the frangipani incensed with night
presses against the curtained window.

Ripples in the basin near the stone wall,
rose petals from evening whirling down:
it's dawn, it's dawn; a pale lawn appears
with the minaret's last cry.

The Last Qawwali

Pakistan, 1971: The watchman fired potshots
in the night when sirens sounded, louder than
a call to prayer from the nearest mosque.
We ran for cover under the dining table.
Mother's re-upholstered chairs
enclosed us like her arms.

We stirred a glue of flour and water,
cut out large sheets of opaque black paper
to block light from escaping our rooms.
We feared the descent into trenches
mandated for civilian lawns
more for the mosquitoes it housed
than for a face to face with an enemy
passed out in the flower bed at dawn.

2016: We lost license for the nostalgia of wartime
songs, the black and white of teary melodies,
of planes gone missing on snowy crags,
soldiers under mud and river stones.
Singers are the martyrs now,
children beg on the road,
tables and chairs piled high for pyres,
no trace left of black papered homes.

Elegy for My Tongue

Ghom are unarticulated words not found; method: erasure.
My *zabaan* was yanked out, not what you'd expect; the hands
of a mullah. The smoothness of my back a map I folded
long ago as a child. I never talked much after that. The circles
he drew grew smaller and smaller, until I diminished to a pebble,
and it was comforting to disappear into the vastness of a lake.
And I'm not sure why I don't mourn my silence.
What I mourn is my native tongue, the one I never had.
I once wrote a letter to my dad, and he mentioned I
had a way with words. I was taught early on that *Angrezi*
is the language my ancestors struggled to learn, when invaded.
Ghayn is the sixteenth of Urdu's thirty-six letter alphabet.
Gham is the sadness my daughters have for losing their mother's tongue.

The Clothesline

All the times you climbed into a tree to hide
way up high, or at least it seemed that way
when you were a quiet child,
and being invisible was easy,
and no one questioned you,
and scraping a knee
or grazing a thigh
while pulling up on this
one branch you preferred
was a choice,
and the ground
became distant, voices
hushed, and you
breathed in the still air,
surveyed your perspective
and returned on days
when the wind howled
and the leaves were
in a terrible commotion
and the clotheslines
violent, flinging clothes
stiff from the sun
into the air like
mammoth butterflies—
and you understood
the power of the wind,
held on to your perch,
unafraid, reveling

that no one knew
this side of you,
while all you ever
really wanted—
was to be found.

On Dry Ground

Sylbiyah, I thought of you
when my daughter broke up
with someone she thought she loved.

You were singing, *parsley sage rosemary and thyme,*
before your father died. Our friends
thought you were too sentimental.

Houston is flooded from the rains.
My grandson places a kiss on my arm.
My granddaughter is nearly one,
and bounces to an MJ song.

Sylbiyah, you passed away
in the measured inches
of a newspaper obituary,
and I knew nothing of it
till a snippet was mailed
to me in an envelope.

Decades since we slipped notes
across the classroom, or walked
the corridors at recess in our
Karachi-Convent schoolgirl uniforms.

Under the shed of a college
courtyard, we nibbled on milk fudge,
four squares for a rupee, and you

told me of your father's cancer.
Much of what you never shared
was held back in your gray-green eyes.

The storm in Houston shut down the city.
Creeks flowed over capacity.
I tie my horses to higher ground,
I keep sweet basil at hand.

After Inhabiting Spaces Where Nothing That Mattered Could Grow

we walked in disbelief
under the arrogance of the trees
                                    the inquiry of leaves
                hush of damp earth
the wind between the rocks
                            lichen and moss
      flecks of sun on fecund rock
                                  and the silence
eavesdropping on our cowering breaths
        My daughters
                          the narrow passage
between the two rock walls
where we hesitated at first
                              then to the verdant stepping stones
the spread of ferns on the forest floor
                      such green rushing towards us

The Reluctant Mourner
for the Refugee Mother

Sometimes the dead choose us
as we stand on the sidelines,
hesitant to give ear to the gaping mouth.

We follow the cavalcade of blinking lights,
wipers swipe,
we brush away tears.

We fixate on the form being lowered to the ground,
the protrusion of a heel from the shroud,
the bend of an elbow,
shoulder grazing the dense chamber of dirt.

Take a handful of dust and fling it thrice.
He who gives life gives death, Habibti.

The rain moves out
but the day remains somber.

A dazzle of sunlight on the cemetery grounds,
the oddness of a breath of air
after closure.

Her children arrange roses and mums, stem side down,
alternating them, unrushed,

as if spacing them out,
or delaying departure,
could generate life on the fresh mound.

Consider the Day

A light washes the garden with the hopefulness
of exchanges,
a blustery wind swings the door open
as if some big hearted soul
walked in
and fall leaves—drained of life—
rain down from the tree
in continuous celebration,
then huddle on the porch,
or chase
in never-ending circles
until lifted by a small gust,
they separate.

The sky is a mother
gathering turnips and heads of lettuce
in her apron,
and so much depends on
the chalk drawings under the walkway,
in the creamy yellows and wavy pinks,
and the joy of hopping
between the lines.

Urdu as Motif: An Elegy in Three Voices

ج *Jeem*

To have a view when the fog allowed,
frolic filtering through windowpanes
from the park across from the house.
To have an affinity for flowers and trees,
to know their botanical names,
to watch the leaves turn glossy,
and petals smitten by the rain.
To be temporary and flitting in the wind.
I grew a lemon tree once, in a house
where doors opened one room
to another like a crossword puzzle—
to have inhabited those empty spaces
without the need for answers.

ل *Laam*

You were home
                             the same day
and through the night—

                To disappear
        into the warmth
                  of your neck

When the river rises to the elevation of the city
        stay with me

                              I will carry you
        into the length and breadth of singularities
                You are   jhumka-bael
                         gulaab
                   raat-ki-raani
                            motia
        haar-singhaar   chumbeli
                         chumpa
                alstonia   on water

م *Meem*

Was it odd to turn the stove off mid-sizzle,
the recipe from a book I turn to time and again,
half a teaspoon of anise, cumin, mustard, nigella
seeds pop and sputter, turmeric, oil splatters.

Was it odd to sit myself down in a chair,
to raise both hands in prayer
and listen to the silence, as if
someone I loved was passing through.

I bear witness—there is no god
but God.

Beloved, holding off death
between isolated breaths,
the door was left open for you.

The Immeasurable Weight of Light

I help my grandson memorize words
for his spelling test.

First grade words: *tell, say, read,*
string, kite, pen, words.

Don't forget the *s* at the end of *words*.
Don't forget.

Paper remembers a steaming cup of black tea
with cardamom and milk,
and the glide of a fountain pen.

Grandfather was a teen when he helped his father
edit and type up survey notes.

At eighty-something my father translates and compiles
his father's memoir,
asks when I will have a book to show.

Paper remembers the strike of a typewriter,
the stroke of a keyboard.

Light from a window conjures floating particles to life.

On Being Asked What Language I Write In

I
Great grandfather made sure his son
got tutored
in a useful tongue.

In 1918, he dedicated his notes
(Page 15-28, Vol. XVII)

To,
The Hon'ble Mr. N
B.A., I.C.S., O.B.E,
Britain's Chief Secretary to the Government
of the Central Provinces of India,
who always sympathized with,
and encouraged the education of…

II
I dedicate this
  to,
    My Honorable Grandfather
    B.A, I.C.S., O.B.E, HPK,
    Chief Secretary,
    and more…

  who,
    was not only held in the highest regard
    for his unswerving desire to serve

ordinary people but was known
for his humility.

III
Thirty years after the bloody partition of India and Pakistan,
he stood in the sweltering verandah of his home in Karachi
and recited a verse from Gray's *Elegy Written in a Country Churchyard*
to his young granddaughter:

> *Far from the madding crowd's ignoble strife*
> > *Their sober wishes ne'er learn'd to stray;*
> *Along the cool, sequester'd way of life*
> > *They kept the noiseless tenor of their way.*

The Reunion at Khayaban-e-Khushi, Karachi

Under the tree, we danced.
The tree in the courtyard between the rooms,

till our shoes hurt, till we kicked our shoes off
and our heels were sore,

till the paint on the makeshift floor
rubbed off on our toes.

We danced because it was winter, and the ixora
was a profusion of red.

We danced because a bulbul built its nest
in the branch of a weeping fig.

Because we knew, once we left,
the tree in the courtyard would shed its leaves again.

Our brothers and their wives, our children,
our nieces and nephews, our cousins

from four continents, danced. We danced
because our darling aunts and uncles were there.

A brother-in-law.
The music.

The night. The lights in the tree.
Our parents' home.

Morning.

٣

The Artificial Lake

It's what they call God's day, my daughter said
as we settled on the grass to watch birds land
on the lake by the neighborhood trail.
Water's starry heads bobbed towards us.

We sat in a grove of new plantings
where pine breezes filled the shade.
The concrete bank lined with moss
melded into water—shadows lengthened.

Spring's almost here, orange paintbrush
and bluebonnets line the ditches,
turtles sit on rocks under bridges,
none of what was given to us.

Remember how we used to point to the sky,
she said, and trace shapes in the clouds.

When December Runs into a Tree of Gold

the earth smacks of decay
though the sun is blinding,
rendering the leaves
a shade of ginger-lemon.
Save for the glitter of a cobweb
in the branches, or the buzz
of an inadvertent fly,
wood chimes mimic eons.

This is how it must feel to die.
Feet blanketed by yesterdays,
face to the sky, I am my four-year-
old granddaughter in ponytails
crunching leaves under my bike.
Summers move through me,
spring clings to flimsy branches,
I am my gray-haired mother
murmuring, I am here, I am here.

Like Homemade

One boy said it was like
cotton candy   moist bits
      on face and arms
warm batter
      splattered on walls
smudged notebooks splayed
in the halls
      From under the desk
the ceiling appeared
      muffin-pocked
the air hard
like taffy at the point of no return
      crackling caramel
the light
of a hundred thousand suns
piercing the classroom window
      maple sugar
when it burns

Back then Houston was like any other city,

the water always level with the street,
lapping on the side of the road like a shoreline.
Some birds made landings in Bear Creek.
Half-submerged trees rose like moorings
as the waters took weeks to recede.

Then more rain and roof claims.
Curbside pickup made special rounds
for moldy carpet and soggy drywall
left out in self-respecting communities.

And all the while the wars on our screens:
the arrests, the daily footage on smart phones,
weeks of limp half-mast flags that otherwise flew
in our faces when we braced our spines
on the curve of highway overpasses
on our way to work and home. On some days

the light just before the rain was a translucence
between sunflower and a tint of green
we wanted to believe in,

and when the sky broke into brilliance
and the low hanging clouds scattered,
we reached up in unison
to gather their soft forms into our arms.

And grandson, you were only three,
but so quiet on our walk home from the mailbox,

your head down, eyes on the road,
because the cicadas were loud in the trees.

By the Broken Obelisk for Dr. King Outside Rothko Chapel in Houston

My daughters and I came upon big soap bubbles
                iridescent
suspendings
                     on loosely looped cords
          plump
     liquid   wobblings
on the reflecting pool's
                impenetrable
dark
                     surface   tilting
          the balance
    wind scattered
               rushings on bamboo

We sat on a bench and watched the afternoon
             reunite with
                    an evening
that would close out
          the years of abandonment

The leaves thought they were rivulets
                      or waterfalls
the way they rippled
and the branches of oaks—
            giant sieves
    salvaging the day
             from the damp ground

Found on the Richter Scale

When was holding on not justifiable:
mantra 2019—#joy.

Weeping is a kind of joy,
unlike remembrance.

Amidst a box of saved birthday cards,
I found a firsthand account
of an earthquake in northern Pakistan,
post 9-11.

"The cold marble floor moved,
the staircase shook
and shivered
horribly,
the chandelier
swayed
like a swing just abandoned by a child."

Within   minutes
               people
   entire
         families
their   modus   operandi.

Do I dare solicit empathy?

Who are we to extricate from the exquisite
entanglements of cement and steel?

Refrigerator   paper   door
knife   trophy   mattress
belt   broom   shoe
bottle   pillow   lamp
book   chair   clock
ring   purse   key

Somewhere, hidden in there
were gardens,
and closets full of rubble
and debris—debris.

Truth Be Told I Did Not Care to Be Taken Aside

to be asked about any accommodations
for fasting in Ramadan, which, by the way,
was months away, and me never bringing it up
or anything, but to think that someone decided
they could map out a litany of my life choices,
and it's not like I do not appreciate intention,
but the assumption that *all* of us love being
crammed into a box like the one they counted
pennies from, but why blame one when profiling
in all its forms is a thing, and what I meant to say
was I am not such an anomaly after all, but instead
I blurted I'm not that virtuous, to which there was
an audible gasp, and after that it was a long, long day.

Texas Toll

On the road again. The vastness of the land,
and the sky a miraculous shield of silver
piercing the storm laden clouds.
To drive into this paradise
without a destination in mind.
A momentary burst of light
brings pale bushes and paler fields
into view before they're delivered
to darkness. Tag sensors flash synapses—
neurons firing, or an angel gone out with a spark?

Thresholds

In Houston's wildlife sanctuary,
baby blue jays eat plump blueberries.
The smell of bird is a sticky green
you can never erase from memory.

Birds love my friend, Mona.
They build nests in her doorway,
returning religiously at beginning of summer.

Mona has taken every bird into her care—
She lets them wander in her hair and nuzzle in her neck.
They vie for her attention.

All the names she's ever given them,
the child in her they bring out. There was Bumble,
the duckling that wandered into her garden
the same night another child
died in custody at the Texas border
without a parent nearby.

Mona forwarded me a video of the little fluffball.
There was Bumble at her forehead,
Bumble on her shoulder,
Bumble on the furniture.

I said, it probably wasn't the smartest thing
to get so close to what's wild.

But what else can you do when a baby bird shows up
at your doorstep?

I sent Mona the link to the Texas Wildlife Refuge on I-10.
They took in all kinds of critters.

I did not tell her
what every other source confirmed:
without its natural mother,
Bumble's chances of survival
were down zero.

Shehr Ashob or Misfortunes of a City

The strength of a city is in its poetry.
Ask an artist, or an architect, and they might say otherwise.

    I saw my uncle, the artist, laughing out his last days
        in a room hung three rows up to the ceiling

    with paintings his English wife, a beloved art critic,
        was gifted by Lahore and Karachi's finest.

Those are cities from whose rubble writers and artists rise.
    I live in a city where I keep out of sight.

The poet Mir's inquiry about the fate of wandering lovers—
    and saba answered by blowing on a fistful of dust—

    nearly slayed me, and I thought
    driving down a Houston highway, vile.

  Be Someone.

    Iconic graffiti on a rustworn pedestrian overpass,
  and a glassy downtown upholds the sky.

    O poets of Mughal Delhi, I survive
amidst the concrete of a crushing workday,

carrying with me your perfectly balanced lines
    of Urdu, a language of unparalleled poetry.

In the neighborhoods you lived, and narrow streets you walked,
not many know of you, though your poems live on.

On the steps of the Jama Mosque, Mir Taqi Mir
exchanged frivolous lines for necessities.

Khwaja Mir Dard, the Sufi poet, danced defiantly,
not surrendering a single verse to patronize royalty.

And Mirza Ghalib, who held Urdu's pulse,
laughed away debt, confident he was for the ages:

*Of course, there are countless talented poets in the world—
but it's said that Ghalib's style is unrivaled.*

O poets of Houston, whose day will you bring to a halt
two hundred years from now?

Let it be known we were not storied like Delhi,
cultured like Lahore, or restless like Karachi,

but this was our city,
and when we met in small bookstores, coffee shops, and bars

tucked away from the crowds, we too were convinced
we had something worth leaving.

saba: the morning breeze

The *Soandhaapun* of Rain on Dry Earth

is indescribable,
and so is the taste and texture
of a halva made of sugar, ghee,
and cracked wheat,
and the burden is not
in the translation,
or the ingredients,
but in pretending
that the word does not exist.

For when the clouds disperse,
and the city returns
to a dust so thick
it is indiscernible,
you can walk around
masking your face.
You can pretend you're incapable
of inhaling, except you reek
of mud and water, and blood and bones,
and the sizzle of water on earth is undeniable.

۵

The Tree by the Garden Gate

A dried pomegranate
rolled out from the trunk as I reached
for a bag of groceries.

I thought I'd removed it with the others last summer,
gift of a woman who could only give.
Plucked a few days before she died,
it was hollow now and rattled when I shook it.

I placed the red fruit on the ledge of the fence
to admire its imperfect form, faded colors,
but it reminded me of a cheek sunken into bone.

Later I searched everywhere
but could not find the dried-up thing.

It had been buried under the wet soil
by exuberant boys who did not know better.
They wanted to dig with the garden shovel
to see if the seeds would grow.

Found Anthem

Skyscrapers will turn   their lights off
                                         stars will spill
like shattered
            glass   warbler and thrush
                                         and sparrow
                                                    wings
will billow like   flags   in the wind
                                         beaks
jammed into brain
at impact   will be reconstructed
            broken bones
                will reset
                                         waxwings
will have eyesight   restored
windows will be
                                                    retro fitted
                                         with red
    white   and blue
decals   there will be no
                                         need for
ziplock bags   no
spatial   disorientation
or delayed arrivals   a single flower
            will be spring
                                         the ruby-
                throated   hummingbird
    will catch the reflection
                                         of its wings
    and   flit   fledglings

78

will find their way   in the dark
there will be   no fatal
            concussions
no search for   dead birds
                nocturnal
                                   songbirds
        will   sing till dawn

Related to the Viscera

When the song played, I forget which one,
a vista lay before me.
Wide-eyed children who knew their futures
were nowhere to be seen.
There were trees—beautiful barks
from which hung crocheted lichen,
and all but a few branches held onto their leaves.
The air was raw, and fine like washed muslin,
and it was impossible to breathe
without taking in Houston's bayous
thick with mud and debris.
I wanted to fill every hour with a poem.
The avenue, glistening with leaves, was irreparable.

Thirty Minute Oil Change in a Free Country

This is the summer of cicadas—I cannot say
tree-trimming is not a worthy aesthetic,
like labeling spice jars, or like these polite
exchanges with a young veteran taken
by the psychedelic swirls of my blouse.
It may all be worth the old couch at Happy Cars,
radiator sizzling between slanted inquiries,
his shaky voice, my unshakeable accent,
his frail frame, trembling hands clutching
a welder's helmet, my taut blouse, his line of sight
aimed at my chest. The banality of an auto shop
in the suburb of a city, his passing remark
about PTSD and six years of service to country.
Add my gratitude, dear boy, I wish you better memories.

Parable

A propitious moon in the tarmacked sky
above the gas station. A halo, hovering
over skeletal branches: it limned
the station's white lights. The glare
from beyond the curb was so blinding,
I almost mistook it for a kitschy heaven.
Lacquer red gas pumps called out,
Come, fall into my arms tonight!
A believer drawn to the glimmer
of story, I pulled in, mindless of cost.

The Unlikeliness of Empty Spaces

The body cannot
sift
memory
into sachets.

One morning I woke to a dove
cooing in the tree outside my window.

One morning I touched
my forehead
to the ground.

How old, the desire
to be held
like a desert
flower on the side
of a knotted stem.

Yesterday, I was
a crowd.
This morning, I woke
to the applause
of a bed.

The desire to be
held, long
after the last drop
has left the flesh.
Water runs where it can.

Let's Talk About the Leaves

Lately, there's been an abundance
lying hapless in the streets,
their curling edges tracing closer
to a web of veins.

A poet
confirmed
that it was considerably safer
to babble on
and on about trees,
study their years,
consider time in the circumference
of their rings, comment vastly on sunlight
falling through crackling branches.

I want to half ignore a finding
that trees too have intention,
care for their offspring, redirect water
through root and rhizome.

As if talking trees were not enough,
now, what little nourishment is left
to ingest guilt-free—gone.

The irony that I came across
the word *bisociation*
at a day job:

apparently incompatible
but uncannily related
frames of reference
leading to discovery.

I take my cue from the leaves,
loss of stem,
separation from branch,
bagged (consider lucky),
left for pickup at the curb.

Texas Blooms

Chrysanthemums bloomed against the indigo sky,
purple petals loomed on the horizon in the windscreen.
The road was a garden, the cars zooming past
were butterflies fluttering in the breeze.
The speed posts were fairy and flamingo stakes,
and the lights above the poles were the kind
that soaked the sun, glowing like fireflies by night.
And there were chimes: wood, copper, and glass
beads that shone and made clunking noises.
My heart was a chrysanthemum pulsing in my chest,
every glorious thud in the road a heady forgetfulness.
A gold pollen dusted the velocity-laden highway

The Donning

It takes time to shed the garments
that are the mark of a new immigrant.
It takes more to begin to understand.
To search for answers—to be an answer.

A stranger shouted at my daughter
(thirty-something) at a grocery store,
"You gorgeous as hell!"
The owner of a small bakery
next to where I worked
told me I looked American,
then asked me where I was from.

When we were kids, my siblings and I waited
for our weekly T.V. shows;
Little House on the Prairie, *The Six Million Dollar
Bionic Man*. We leapt
from chairs
in slo-mo, begged our parents
to buy us more *Archie* comic-books.

Yes, even as we were growing up
in places
our grandfathers fought for,
the allure of a Jim or Jenny
was never far. We
wondered what

Hostess twinkies were like;
what made an *American*?

Perhaps, now I walk with confidence—
no, an arrogance—
that is gorgeous, hell, America.

I Close my Eyes and Stand Under the Tallow

and listen to the wind
                              that ripples through its branches
    xylophonic leaves
                    tattered prayers
    abandoned
                    in the foothills of the Himalayas
thoughts
        luminous
                where shadows intervene
like kisses
        on forehead
                eyes
                          cheek
woodwinds stir the ground beneath
                          face turns up
        to greet the green

Acknowledgments

My gratitude to the editors of these journals where these poems, or an earlier version, first appeared, some with different titles.

Arc Poetry: "Truth Be Told I Did Not Care to Be Taken Aside"

The Aleph Review: "My Karachi and the Sea"

The Bangalore Review: "The Remuneration"

Barrow Street: "A Nearly Dried-Up Woman"

Cimarron Review: "The Tree by the Garden Gate"

Equinox Hot Poet: "After Inhabiting Spaces Where Nothing That Matters Could Grow," "Texas Tag"

Glass: A Journal of Poetry: "The Artificial Lake"

Jaggery: "The Prayer"

Natural Bridge: "The Geometry of an Ellipse"

On the Seawall: "The Kite," "The Unlikeliness of Empty Spaces"

Puerto del Sol: "Related to the Viscera," "Urdu as Motif: An Elegy in Three Voices"

Reunion: The Dallas Review: "The Resettlement"

Sequestrum: "Consider the Day," "The Reluctant Mourner," "When December Turns into a Tree of Gold"

Texas Review: "Ya Allah Ya Rabb"

"On Dry Ground" and "Thresholds" were published in *Eco Poetry: Odes and Elegies from the Texas Gulf Coast*, ed. Katherine Hoerth (Lamar University Press, 2020).

"Like Homemade," was published in *Enchantment of the Ordinary*, ed. John Gorman (Mutabilis Press, 2018).

"Back then Houston was like any other city," was published in *Kill Line*, ed. Kalen Rowe (Anklebiters Publishing, 2017).

"A Nearly Dried-up Woman," "The Resettlement," and "The Tree by the Garden Gate" were reprinted in *Sequestrum*.

"Like Homemade" was featured in *Sappho's Torque* on April 19, 2019.

"The Geometry of an Ellipse" (as "The Other Immigrants") was featured in *Synkroniciti* on March 3, 2016.

"The Missing Planet was featured in *Sappho's Torque* on April 30, 2022.

"The Missing Planet" was featured in *The Houston Chronicle* and *The San Antonio Express-News* on July 25, 2021.

"Texas Tag" was the winner of the Hot Poet Spring Equinox: Volume II Poetry Contest in 2022.

My immense gratitude to Cait Weiss Orcutt for her brilliant guiding light, dynamism, and confidence in my work; my manuscript would not have gotten this far without her edits, prompts, and gracious feedback. Many thanks to Brandi George for her warm feedback and words of encouragement. Thank you to my University of Houston professors: Ange Mlinko, Martha Serpas, and Kevin Prufer, in whose classes some of these poems began. Thank you to my fellow poets in Cait's class for their reading and feedback: Elina Melinger, Elisabeth Commanday Swim, Emily Bludworth de Barrios, Miah Arnold, and Tamara Nicholl-Smith. Thank you to

Analicia Sotelo and my University of Houston peers for their friendship and support. Thank you to Patricia McMahon, Rebecca Danelly, and Varsha Saraiya-Shah for their love, support, and friendship. Many thanks to my publisher, Diane Lockward, for bringing my book into the world.

I am grateful to all those Houston poets and organizers who have featured me in the spaces they created for poetry to be read or heard. Thank you to all my instructors and peers in the many workshops I have taken. My gratitude to the Mutabilis Press team, Angélique Jamail, Chuck Wemple, Matt Riley, and Yolanda Movsessian for their support. To the large family of Houston's community of poets, thank you for your love and support.

Much gratitude to Saif Mahmood for his book *Beloved Delhi: A Mughal City and Her Greatest Poets* which was a source of inspiration for "Shehr Ashob or Misfortunes of a City." Much gratitude to Dr. Mohammad Haroon Siddiqui, for allowing me to borrow a couplet from his book of poems, *Mein Sochta Rehta Hoon*. Much love and gratitude to Yasmin Akbar-Husain and my father for inviting me to co-edit my grandfather's memoir, *Memoirs of a Very Civil Servant: Akhter Husain*, which was a source of inspiration for several poems in this collection. A special thanks to Naila for helping me with my book.

Finally, thank you to my beautiful siblings and their spouses for their unwavering love and support, my darling daughters and their families for their love and support, and the joys they share with me and my loving parents, Ishrat and Zahid Husain, who move through life with grace, elegance, and above all, kindness.

About the Author

Saba Husain is a Pakistani-born American poet. Her poems can be found in literary journals, including *Barrow Street*, *Cimarron Review*, *Third Coast*, and *On the Seawall*. Earlier versions of this manuscript were chosen as a 2023 Perugia Press Prize finalist, as well as a 2021 and 2020 X.J. Kennedy Poetry Prize finalist. Her awards include first place in the 2022 Spring Equinox Hot Poet Poetry Contest, the 2020 Editor's Choice Award from Lamar University Press and the Center for History and Culture, and the 2014 Lorene Pouncey Award at the Houston Poetry Fest. She holds a day job and has served on the board of Mutabilis Press since 2019. She earned a Bachelor of Arts in Creative Writing from the University of Houston. *Elegy for My Tongue* is her first full-length poetry collection.